DAY TRADING

STRATEGIES CRASH

COURSE

THE ULTIMATE DAY TRADING CRASH COURSE. DISCOVER HOW TO MAKE MONEY IN 7 DAYS AS A BEGINNER OR ADVANCED TRADER MOST POWERFUL STRATEGIES AND LEARN THE PSYCHOLOGY BEHIND THIS ACTIVITY

Benjamin Ray Bears

MORNING STAR

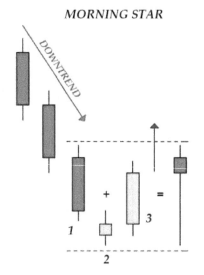

EVENING STAR

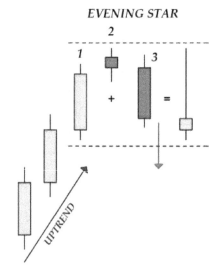

HAMMER	Bullish		A N A L I S I	**SHOOTING STAR**	Bearish	
INVERTED HAMMER	Bullish			**HANGING MAN**	Bearish	
BULLISH ENGULFING	Bullish			**BEARISH ENGULFING**	Bearish	
TWEEZER BOTTOMS	Bullish		C A N D L E S T I C K	**TWEEZER TOP**	Bearish	
MORNING STAR	Bullish			**EVENING STAR**	Bearish	
THREE WHITE SOLDIERS	Bullish			**THREE BLACK CROWS**	Bearish	
THREE INSIDE UP	Bullish			**THREE INSIDE DOWN**	Bearish	

Table of Contents

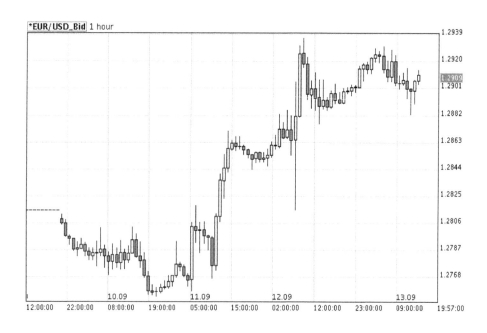

Introduction

T here is often confusion about why traders choose options when stocks and bonds do just fine. What some tend to miss out on is the vast difference in the earnings potential. Stocks generally return a profit of 8%–12% per annum, which is pretty impressive in and of it. However, options are a lot more lucrative with a much larger potential.

Firstly, options' flexibility allows them to be traded based on a wide variety of underlying securities. The variety and range of options strategies are massive. Also, the spreads provide real flexibility in the manner in which they can be traded. Traders have flexibility and versatility in limiting the risks of assuming market positions when it comes to hedging. Even simply trying to benefit from stock movements, there are numerous opportunities available.

Some options trades typically generate profits upwards of 50%. Making 100% profits within a short period and even more, is not unheard of. This is why a lot of experienced traders choose options. They are extremely lucrative and highly profitable. It is also possible to make money trading options in any market condition. Traders can make money when the market is bullish, bearish, and even when it is stagnant. As such, you do not need specific market conditions, and hence profitability throughout the year is possible.

Experts agree that trading options offer plenty of benefits that are not offered by other types of securities. While not all traders may want to engage in options trading, there are certain aspects of it that other traders find attractive.

Potential for Astronomical Profits

One of the main reasons for trading options is the opportunity of making significantly large profits compared to all other forms of trade in the markets. This is possible even without large sums of money. The principle behind this approach is leverage. A trader needs not to have large amounts of funds to earn huge profits. For instance, with as little as $10,000, it is possible to earn amounts such as $300,000 or even $800,000 simply using leverage.

Take the example of a trader whose trading fund is $10,000. The trader wishes to invest this amount in Company ABC. Now the current stock price is $20 though this price is expected to rise. The trader could use the funds to purchase the shares directly and receive 500 shares for their money. If the stock price were to rise to $25 within a month, the trader would have made $5 per share or a total of $2,500 in profits.

Alternatively, the trader could purchase call options of XYZ stocks with the same amount of money. The options allow the trader to purchase back the underlying stocks within a certain period. Now, options contracts cost between $1 and $4 depending on certain factors, such as the underlying security value. In our example, one call options costs $2 so for the $10,000, the trader receives 5,000 options contracts.

If the trader chooses to exercise the right to sell the underlying shares in the next month, they stand to profit from $5 per share. Remember that they have a right to a total of 5,000 shares for a total profit of $25,000. This demonstrates the capacity and power of options and how profitable this kind of trade can be.

Versatility and Flexibility

Another extremely appealing benefit of trading in options is the inherent flexibility. Options offer lots of flexibility with dozens of different strategies to pursue. This compares well with numerous other trade and investment options out there. Most of these do not offer as much flexibility as options do. Also, most other securities have limited strategies, limiting the flexibility that a trader has on that security.

Take stocks, for instance. Even stock traders encounter certain limitations that are not inherent in options trading. There are plenty of strategies ranging from simple to compound to complex strategies. Stock traders generally buy, hold, or sell stocks. This contrasts greatly with options because of the tens of strategies available to them. The versatility and flexibility inherent in options trading far surpass that of most other securities.

Great Risk vs. Reward Consideration

Like all good traders, it is essential to weigh the risk posed by a certain trade compared to the possible rewards. When trading using options, the style adapted will indicate the type of risk inherent in the trade. The above example clearly shows how profitable the options trading process is. If a loss were to be incurred in the above instance, then the total loss would have been the options' cost.

In this case, the risk is worth the reward because the amount expected to be lost negligible compared to the gain to be made. In general, the higher the risk than the higher the potential return. Any time a trader considers a trade, then the risk versus reward ratio should be considered.

Chapter 1: Stepping Up a Tier: Buying Calls

B uying calls is a more advanced form of training than selling covered calls. But it's not that complicated, so let's dive in.

What You're Actually Buying

Remember that one option contract is for 100 shares, so you'll need to be able to buy 100 shares of the stock in order to exercise your right to buy.

Also, remember that an options contract has a deadline. If the stock price fails to exceed the strike price by the deadline, you're out of luck and will lose whatever money that you invested in the premium. In relative terms, the premium price will be small, so chances are if you are careful and not starting out by buying large numbers of options contracts, you won't be out that much money.

Your Goal Buying Options Contracts

The goal when purchasing options contracts is to buy a stock at a price that is lower than its current market value. In other words, you want the stock price to be significantly higher than the strike price so that you're enjoying significant savings in purchasing the stock. When evaluating your options, you'll need to consider the added costs of the premium paid plus commissions. In some cases, commissions can be substantial, so make sure you know what they are ahead of time so that you choose a good strike price and exercise your options at the right time.

You're a Trader, Not an Investor

You may be mentally conditioned to think in terms of investing. An investor wants to build a diversified portfolio over a long time period that they believe will increase in value over the long term. Traders operate in the same way but have different objectives. They are looking for short-term profits, not investments because they will not hold these stocks. If you were interested in holding the stock, you would simply buy it at the lower price that is currently on offer. Your goal is to be able to buy at the strike price when the stock has increased significantly in price and then sell it immediately so that you can pocket the profits.

Let's take an example. Suppose that XYZ Corporation is currently selling at $30 a share. People are expecting the stock to rise, and some people are really bullish about its short-term prospects. If you are an investor, your goal is to get the stock at the lowest possible price and then hold it long-term. If you are using strategies like dollar-cost averaging, you might be buying a few shares every month without paying too much attention to what the price is specifically on the day you purchase. In any case, as an investor, you'll simply buy the shares at $30.

As a trader, you're hoping to cash in on the moves of XYZ over the next couple of months. You'll buy an options contract; let's say its premium is $0.90 and the strike price is $35. Your cost for the 100 shares is $90.

Then the stock price shoots up to $45. Since it passed the strike price, you can exercise your option to buy the shares at the strike price. You can buy them at $35 for a total price of $3,500. But remember—you're not an investor in for the long haul. You'll immediately unload the shares. You sell the shares for $4,500 and make a $1,000 profit. After considering your premium, your profit is $910. It will go a little bit lower after considering commissions, but you get the idea. The purpose of buying call options is to make fast profits on stocks you think are going to spike.

It's hard to guess when the best time is to really buy call options. Obviously, you don't want to do it when a major recession hit. The optimal time is during a bull market, or when a specific company is expected to hit on something big that will suddenly increase its value in the markets. A good time to look is also when a recession hits, but it passes the bottom out period.

Benefits of Buying Call Options

Call options have many benefits that we've already touched on earlier. In Particular:

- Call options allow you to control 100 shares of stock without actually investing in the 100 shares—unless they reach a price where you get the profit that you want.
- Call options allow you to sit and wait, patiently watching the market before making your move.
- If your bet doesn't work out, you're only going to lose a small amount of money on the contract. In our example, if XYZ loses value, and ends up at $28 per share instead of moving past your strike price of $35, then you're only out the $90 you paid for the premium.
- Call buying provides a way to leverage expensive stock.

What to Look for When Buying Call Options

Now let's take a look at some factors that you'll be on the lookout for when buying call options. You're going to want to be able to purchase shares of the stock you're interested in at a price that is less than the price you think it will go up to. You need to do this in order to ensure that the stock price surpasses the strike price. Of course, it's impossible to know what the future holds, so this will involve a bit of speculation. You'll have to do a lot of reading and research to make educated guesses on where you expect the stock to go in the next few weeks or months.

Second, you'll need to consider the cost of the premium when making your estimates. For the sake of simplicity, suppose that you find a call option with a premium of $1 per share. You're going to need a strike price that is high enough to take that into account. If you go for a stock that is $40 a share with a $1 premium and a strike price of $41, obviously, you're not going to make anything unless the stock price goes higher than $41.

Remember that exercising your rights on the options contract is not a path toward immediate money. You're going to have to turn around and sell it ASAP in order to profit. Of course, when you sell is a judgment call, as is when you exercise your right to buy. You're going to want to wait until the right moment to buy, but it's impossible to really know what that right moment is. This is where trading experience helps and even then, the most skilled experts can make mistakes. For a beginner, the best thing to do is exercise your right to buy the shares and then sell them as soon as they've gone far enough past the strike price for you to make a profit and cover the premium. If you wait too long, there is always the chance that the stock price will start declining again, and it will go below your strike price and never exceed it again before the contract expires.

Open Interest

If you get online to check stocks you're interested in, one of the measures you will see is "Open Interest." This tells you the number of open or outstanding derivative contracts there are for that particular stock. Every time that a buyer and seller enter into an options contract, this value increases by one. What you want to do with open interest as a trader looking to make real cash from call options is to look for stocks that show big movement in the number of open trades. You're going to want to look for increasing numbers. This means that other traders have an interest in buying call options on this stock and that they're expecting it to go up in value in the near future.

Of course, you're going to want to take an educated approach to this. Simply getting online and going through random stocks will be a waste of time, it might take you weeks to find something.

You're going to want to prepare ahead of time by keeping an eye on the financial news. Watch Fox Business, read the Wall Street Journal, and watch CNBC and read any other financial publications that are to your liking. Find out what stocks the experts are talking about and which ones they expect to make significant moves over the next few weeks and months. Keep in mind these people and experts often make mistakes, so you're only using it as a guideline. You also don't want to focus solely on looking for stocks that are going to make moves; you want to keep up with company news. You need to keep your ears open for news such as the development of a new drug or the latest electronic gadget. Sometimes you might find out news about that before the stock begins attracting a lot of interest in the markets.

Chapter 2: Strategies for Buying Calls

Tips for Buying Call Options

- Do not buy a call option with a strike price that you do not think the stock can beat.

- Always include the premium price in your analysis.

- Look for calls that are just in the money. These are likely to bring a modest profit.

- Call options that are out of the money might give you an opportunity for a cheaper premium.

- However, the premium should not be your primary consideration when looking to buy a call option. Compared to the money required to purchase the shares and the potential profits if the stock goes past the strike price, the premium is going to be a little cost in most cases—provided, of course, the strike price is high enough to take the rebate into account.

- Look at the time value. If you are looking for more substantial profits, it is better to aim for more extended contracts. Remember that with any call option you have the opportunity to buy the stock at the strike price at any time between today's date and the deadline when the stock market price exceeds the strike price. More extended time frames mean you increase the chances of that happening.

Even if the price goes a little above the strike price and dips down, with a longer window of time before the deadline, you can wait and see if it rebounds. Remember, if it never does, you are only out the premium.

- Start small. Beginning traders should not bet the farm on options. You will end up broke if you do that. The better approach is to start by investing in one contract at a time and gaining experience as you go.

- The best-case scenario for you, as the buyer, is that the stock suddenly starts rising at high speed before the deadline arrives. You want it to go beyond the strike price so that, when it comes time to exercise your right, you are purchasing your stock at a lower rate than it is now worth. Obviously, you then have the option to instantly list that stock as a covered sell, which would allow you to realize that profit in real money.

- That final piece of the puzzle is the important one. As an options trader, you are not in the business of building a stock portfolio. You do not really want to own those shares – you want to make a profit on them as they pass through your hands. You want to buy them for less than they are worth and then sell them on, perhaps even for more than they are worth if you are lucky. It is within that transaction your money will be made.

Buying calls has several advantages for you as an options trader:

- It does not cost much to get involved in the movement of a stock. You only need to fork out the amount for the premium, after which you can sit back and wait to see what the stock does before making your purchase decision based on actual information, rather than on speculating what the market will do.

- It allows you to make use of the kinds of "tips" that market experts have a terrible habit of swearing by. You read the news, watch the markets, and have information that makes you think an individual stock is about to rise fast and hard. Obviously, you want to take advantage of that, and options trading allows you to do so much more safely than merely buying the stock. If you are wrong, you will only lose your premium and you may even make a small profit. If you were wrong and purchased the stock and then it plummeted rather than rose, you stand to lose a whole lot more cash.

Chapter 3: Understanding Volatility

There's one final factor that affects the prices of contracts on a fundamental basis, though it's not something we've touched on so far. However, the volatility of a contract is an incredibly important concept to grasp for an options trader.

What is Volatility?

Volatility refers to the movement of the underlying stock. Some stocks will slowly wend their way up and down in a predictable manner—those are not very volatile. Others charge on a day-to-day basis and change between up and down along the way.

To sum up the effect of volatility in a single sentence: the more volatile the stock, the more that an options trader is willing to pay for it. A volatile stock has a better chance of reaching the strike price and perhaps shooting far beyond it before the expiration date.

However, it's also the most dangerous of the factors that you need to bear in mind because it's arguably the most likely one to force you into a bad decision. A volatile stock, for example, can lead to a much higher premium and therefore a higher contract price; unless that stock shoots through the roof, you could end up losing money even when you should be making it.

One way to estimate a stock's volatility is to take a look at what it has done in the recent past. This tells you how much it has moved up and down already, which some use as an indicator of how much it will move up and down in the future.

Unfortunately, it's not always true that the past repeats itself, and you can't predict the future based on what's already happened. Instead, options traders use "implied volatility" to make their guesses: the value that the market believes the option is worth.

You can see this reflected in the activity on the options for that stock. Buyers will be keen to get their hands-on options before a certain event takes place, such as the announcement of a new product or a release about the company's earnings. Because of this, options increase in price because there is implied volatility—the market thinks the stock is going to shoot up.

You'll see lower demand on a stock that's flat or moving gently because there is no implied volatility and, therefore no hurry to get in on the action. You'll also see correspondingly low prices for the option.

Volatility is a good thing—as a buyer, you want the stock to be volatile because you need it to climb to the strike price and beyond. However, there is also such a thing as too much volatility. This is when contracts become popular, prices rise up, and you stand to pay more for a contract than you will eventually earn.

Your brokers will likely be able to provide you with a program that will help you determine implied volatility, asking you to enter certain factors and then calculating it for you. However, it's only through experience that you'll learn how to spot a stock that's just volatile enough to justify its higher price—again, practice is the key.

It's also worth noting that a lot of the risk in options trading comes from volatility, largely because it's impossible to be accurate in your estimates. What happens if an earthquake destroys that company's headquarters? Stocks are going to plummet, and you had absolutely no way to see it coming.

That's why options traders are forced to accept that their fancy formulas are not going to be perfect predictors. They will help, but you should still be conservative in your trading and avoid the temptation to sink everything into a trade you believe could make your fortune thanks to its volatility.

Strategies for a Volatile Market

- Long Straddle

This strategy is essentially an amalgamation of the long call and long put trading strategies. You will be using the money options for executing the strategy. You are required to purchase at the money calls along with at the money puts of the same amount. Execute both these transactions simultaneously and ensure that the expiry date for them stays the same. Given that the expiry date is long-term, it gives the underlying security sufficient time to show a price movement and increases your chances of earning a profit. A short-term expiration date doesn't provide much scope for any changes in the price of an asset, so the profitability is also relatively low.

- Long Strangle

This is also known as the strangle strategy, and you must place simultaneous orders with your broker. You must purchase calls on relevant security and then by the same number of puts on the security. The options contracts you execute must be out of the money and must be made simultaneously. The best way to go about it is to purchase those securities that are just out of the money instead of ones that are far out of the money. Make sure that the strike prices in both these transactions are equidistant from the existing trading price of the underlying asset.

- Strip Straddle

This strategy is quite similar to a long straddle- you will be purchasing at the money calls and the money puts. The only difference is that the number of puts you purchase will be higher than the calls your purchase. The expiry date and the underlying asset for both these transactions you make will be the same. The only factor upon which your profitability lies is in the ratio of puts to calls you use. The best ratio is to purchase two puts for every call you make.

- Strip Strangle

You stand to earn a profit if the underlying asset makes a big price movement in either direction is. However, your profitability increases if the price movement is downwards instead of upwards. You will be required to purchase out of the money calls and out of the money puts. Ensure that the number of money puts you make are greater than the out of the money calls you to decide to make. So, to begin with, the ratio of 2:1 will work well for you.

- Strap Straddle

This is quite similar to the long straddle strategy- you are required to purchase at the money calls along with at the money puts for the same date of expiry. You are required to purchase more calls than ports, and the basic ratio to start with is 2:1. User strategy with certainty that there will be an upward movement in the underlying asset price rather than a downward price movement.

- Strap Strangle

This is quite similar to the Long strangle strategy and uses it when you're quite confident that there will be a dramatic movement in the price of the underlying strategy. You tend to earn a profit if the price moves in either direction, but your profitability increases in the price movement are upward. There are two transactions you must execute—purchase out of the money puts and purchase out of the money calls options. However, the number of out-of-the-money calls you to make must be greater than the out-of-the-money puts. The ratio of out of the money puts out-of-the-money calls must be two to one. So, you will essentially be purchasing twice as many calls as sports.

- Long Gut

You are required to purchase in-the-money call options along with an equal number of in-the-money put options. All of these will be based on the same underlying security along with the same date of expiration. The decisions you are required to make while using the strategy are related to the strike price you want to use and the date of expiration. It is suggested that to increase your profitability and reduce the upfront costs, the strike price you must opt for must be closely related to the current trading price of the underlying asset.

- Call Ratio Back Spread

You are required to purchase calls and the right calls to create a call ratio back spread. Since it is a ratio spread, the number of options you execute in each of these transactions will not be the same. As a rule of thumb, try to purchase two calls for every call you write. Always ensure that the total credit for the contracts you've written must be higher than the total debit for the contracts you have acquired.

- Put Ratio Back Spread

You will earn a profit if the price of the underlying asset moves in either direction; however, your profitability increases if the price of the underlying asset price goes down instead of going up. You are required to purchase puts and write puts simultaneously. As is obvious, both of these transactions will be based on the same underlying asset. The only difference is that instead of purchasing an equal number of puts, you will be purchasing to puts for every put you right. The puts you purchase must be at the money while the ones you write must be in the money. The expiry date, along with the underlying security, must be the same.

- Short Calendar Call Spread

The strategy is best used when you are certain that there will be a significant price movement in the value of the underlying security. However, you are uncertain of the direction in which the security will swing. Instead of spending a lot of time trying to analyze the direction of the price change, you can use the strategy. The strategy is likely complicated, and beginners must not attempt it on the first try. There are two transactions you must make.

The first transaction is to purchase at the money calls, and the second transaction is to write at the money calls. Since it is a calendar spread, the expiry date is used for both these transactions must be different. The options you decide to purchase must be short-term with a relatively close expiry date while the options you write must be long-term with a longer date of expiration.

- Short Calendar Put Spread

Two transactions are required to execute this strategy- purchase at the money puts while writing at the money puts. The date of expiration for both these transactions will be different since it is a calendar spread. The price of the contracts that have a longer expiry date will be quite high as compared to the ones with a shorter expiration date. It is based on the basic idea that a substantial movement in the value of the underlying security will mean that the extrinsic value of both sets of options will end up being equal or close to being full. The initial credit you receive is because of the higher extrinsic value of the options written. So, if the extrinsic value becomes equal on both sites, then that credit that will be created is your profits.

Chapter 4: How to Buy and Sell Puts

L et's talk about buying and selling puts. Puts, of course, allow you to sell the stock that you have or the underlying commodity that you have underneath it all. There are different reasons why people may want to buy or sell puts, and here we'll go over what it is, how to do it, and the advantages of such.

What are Buying and Selling Puts?

Selling/buying puts essentially is giving someone the option to buy the stock at a certain amount of money.

If you sell a put option, you're selling the chance for someone to buy that stock at a price.

If you buy a put option, you're giving someone the opportunity to buy that stock for that price and the person is obligated to sell it.

So, let's say that you're planning on getting a put option to buy that stock at a certain amount of money. You can put that option down, and from there, wait for it to fall, and from there, you can exercise it. Maybe you want to buy shares from an outstanding railroad company. You mainly notice it's increasing the earnings on this, and you decide to buy the stock when it's under 30 potentially. By purchasing a put option, basically makes the seller obligated to sell you the stock when it falls below 30 dollars.

You want to exercise these in falling markets since you'll generate a profit when the market is falling rather than rising.

Selling Puts in this Market

Here's the thing, when you want to sell puts, you should only do so if you're comfy with the owning stock that's under it at the price that's there because essentially, you're assuming the obligation to buy it if the person does decide to sell. From this, you should also only enter trades where the net price paid for the security is reasonable. This is the most crucial part of selling puts profitably in the markets that you have. There are other reasons to sell it to the person. You also can own the security below the market price that is currently there, and you'll definitely want to be careful when you do choose to sell this.

An Example of Buying a Put

Let us now move onto buying these puts. One thing to note is that you're not going to see the commissions, taxes, margins, and other charges factored into any of these equations for a reason. That starts to get it a bit more complicated, and right now, we are just showing you the cut and dry of all of the ways you can buy a put option that can be considered. But you should definitely consult with your tax advisor or broker before you go in.

So, let's say you've got company A, which is overvalued currently at $50 bucks a share, and you decide to bet on a decline at this point, getting a put contract that's at $35 a share, and it costs $2 per share, so the "breakeven" price is $33 a share. This is deduced from basic math since you're taking the contract price of 35 minus the 2 making it $33 for this. Since each of these represents 100 different shares, that's $3500 in a total of what you'll buy, and then of course, it'll cost you upfront $200 for this (cause of the options contract and the shares) and from there, you enter the trade.

Now, let's say that the option contract is for August 2019, and from there, you fast-forward and watch the market. Below is a table of what can happen:

Action of stock what happens to you your return Outlook

Soars all the way up to $60. The option expires, becomes worthless, and you lose the $200 premium, but you're basically losing nothing else (100%) Okay Falls slightly to $38. The same thing happens, stock falls but you don't make a profit (100%) Okay Drops all the way to $25 you make some cash! 800 dollars to be exact ($35-25) and then the $2 premium (800%) Nice! Drops to $0 (basically going bankrupt) the ideal situation, and you'll get $3300 from it (0 at expiration, so 3500-200 from the premium) (1500%) Ideal!

So, the best time to use these is when you have a sinking ship in terms of stock. Otherwise, they aren't worth your time, and it's better not to have these stocks, and there is always a chance you could end up losing money. But, if the person sells the capital, and you turn around and cash in on it, you'll have more money, and you don't have to worry about the burden of a stock.

If you choose to buy it when it declines, you're mostly going to get money from this. You want to do it when it's falling and nothing more. It is imperative that you don't choose to act on these types of options until it's that time.

That's it, that's all buying put options is, and you want to make sure that it falls to the level that you want it to be at.

The Risks of It

Risks are still there in both cases. Options are risky due to the complex nature of this, but once you know how these works, it can reduce the risk a whole lot. Put options, in particular, can be quite risky, especially for the seller, since they may have to spend more money buying back the opportunity that they once had.

One other aspect of this, especially for buyers is the break-even aspects of it. So, let's assume that you got a stock today for $46 and this was at $44, which is two points down what it is there, so you'll be profitable in the trade. But here's the thing, you're going to end up losing out on money due to the fee for the option. It would make the option worth $2 since you spent $4 on it, so that means you're losing out on it.

But there is also the fact that if the option does expire and you're in-the-money, you'll get the right stock immediately. You may not realize it, but these can be quite good, especially for plunging markets, especially if you know they will bounce back.

If you end up seeing it go high, you're going to end up paying for that premium to get the right to buy it, and that's money that can rack up to a couple of thousand dollars. Do make sure that you understand that when you do choose to figure out your own stock, and how you can quickly rectify it.

The Advantages of Buying Puts

Buying puts, which give you an option to sell the stock at a given price, is useful if you're looking to protect yourself. So, let's say that you have this stock, or you've been eyeing a share that will probably fall, and then rise over the ensuing few months. There are those out there, and usually, it's due to lulls in the market at the time. So, you decide to buy the put that's there, which gives you the option to sell that stock when the market decides to resurface at a higher level.

For you, you're taking a gamble on this, because the market may not recover, but if you notice a stock that could potentially have the power to fall possibly, this may be a good one. That way, you can get the share for cheaper. From there, you can sell the stock again, and you have the right to sell that stock at the price that you're looking for.

It essentially allows you to form that extra security in his, which is a great little advantage for the person who wants to sell it. Long puts are suitable for this, especially if you're going to sell these.

Put options let you sell this asset at the strike price that's there. With this, the seller is then obligated to purchase these shares from the holder. Now, how can this help? Let's say that you buy a stock at 20 bucks, and then you compare it to 20 dollars at the edge that's there. If the price is below 20 at any point, you can actually then exercise the options and reduce the losses. This can definitely help, especially if you're willing to buy a choice, and from there, sell it in order to avoid lots of trouble.

Naked Puts

There are also naked puts, which is an advanced put options strategy, so I don't suggest trying this until you've worked with basic puts. The reason for that is because of their incredibly risky.

What does it mean to trade an option naked though? It doesn't mean that you're going to the stock exchange in the buff, but rather, you're selling the options without having a position in the underlying instrument. For example, if you're writing a naked put, you're selling a put without having the stock.

The covered call is probably the most basic stock trading strategy. This strategy provides an ideal entry point for those who are new to options trading and allows them to turn their existing investment activities into a gateway for trading options. The premise of the covered call is quite simple. The idea behind this strategy is to minimize your cost basis on your stock purchases.

Let's take a look at how this works.

Covered Call Strategy

The best way to think about a covered call is to look at it as a method to earn dividends on your stock holdings. While a stock may or may not pay you a profit, with a covered call strategy you can earn income on the position and therefore lower your valid purchase price. Another way of looking at this is to view it as turning your stock purchase into a bond that pays you monthly or bi-monthly interest.

So how does it work? Well, the strategy has two legs to it.

- A long stock
- A short call

Execution

The long stock leg is simply your investment purchase in a stock. A lot of people who get into trading already hold shares as part of a retirement account or some other portfolio. If you already own a position in some stock, then employing this strategy will work wonders for you.

The execution is pretty straightforward. You already hold great stock or establish a long stock position in some company that you think has good long-term prospects. I must emphasize that this leg is all about investment and it has nothing to do with speculation. Whatever research you do to purchase this stock should be done on the basis of sound investment principles. So, you need to be aware of the earning ability of the company and its long-term prospects. Do not purchase a stock just to execute a covered call.

The short call simply provides short-term income against your long-term holding. So really, it's an appendage to the original position and gives you some cash in the short term while you're invested for the long-term capital gain. I know I'm repeating myself here, but this is because a lot of beginners think a covered call is a speculative strategy.

Chapter 5: Strategies for New Options Traders

There is no perfect trading strategy; so, stop searching for one. Moreover, you do not need a perfect trading strategy to make money from trading stocks. Ultimately, your trading strategy will be unique to you. However, as a beginner, you may need to lean a bit on an existing strategy to get the hang of it. With time, you can tweak things around to fit your trading style or build yours completely from scratch.

Here is a general idea you can use to build your own trading strategy.

Preparation

You could start preparing for your trade at the beginning of a new week. Find out what types of trade (short or long) you will want to focus on. You could use a technical indicator such as the moving averages to determine this. After that, look at a few financial columns or news, reports, etc. This will give you a general outlook of how stocks are performing and what the market is up to. Look at charts of various industries to see stock strengths and weaknesses, plus promising stocks. Be sure to write down whatever catches your attention in your trading notepad (you don't have one yet?) because in the heat of trading, most things you note mentally won't come to your mind.

Finding Stocks

- Begin to search for potential trades by looking for stocks that:
- Have a strong trend
- Have shown first pullbacks or rallies
- Are at a resistance or support level
- Are in the second or fourth stages
- Are repeatedly touching a support or resistance area

If you do not find a trade that you are comfortable with as a beginner, please do not trade. Remember, trading involves going long, short, or staying in cash. So, learn to stay in cash if there is nothing appealing for you to trade.

Double-Check

After you have found a trade, verify that the company whose stock you are about to trade will not release its earnings reports anytime soon. Trading a company's stock just before their earnings report is released can lead to a massive loss for you. So be sure to double-check. Here's one way you could find out. Simply go to Yahoo Finance and type in the company's symbol. The date of the next earnings report will be shown.

During Trades

All things checked and verified, start your trade. Do not give your attention to stock market news or other trader's opinions during your own trades. Your attention needs to be only in one place: the stock chart. Ensure that you use trailing stops to follow your profits closely and that would be all you require during trades.

Your Entry Strategy

Your money is at risk as soon as you enter a position to buy or sell a stock.

So, you must be careful that you time your entry very well.

Your entry point should be at a swing point: a low swing point for buying, and a high swing point for selling.

A swing point is made up of three candles.

Low Swing Point (for entering a long position – buying)

1. Candle one goes low
2. Candle two goes lower than candle one (lower low)
3. Candle three goes higher than candle two (higher low)

Candle three indicates that sellers are no more aggressive. This is a precursor for a trend reversal. This is your cue to enter a long position.

High Swing Point (for entering a short position – selling)

1. Candle one goes high
2. Candle two goes higher than candle one (higher high)
3. Candle three goes lower than candle two (lower high)

Candle three indicates that buyers are no more aggressive. This is a precursor for a trend reversal. This is your cue to enter a short position.

Successive Up Days or Down Days

Another way to enter a trade is to look for successive up days or down days. These are a lot easier to spot but be sure that you are not entering the trade when the trend is about to end or reverse.

Your Exit Strategy

You have read all the charts and picked your stocks to trade and you have determined which market to trade on—in fact, you know exactly when to time your entry. But when do you exit a trade? When do you lock in profits? You see, as important as timing your entry is, if you neglect when to exit, you may not take any profits home after all.

You must plan well ahead of your entry how you intend to exit a trade. And remember that a plan is not a plan until it is written down. Following a plan in your head is the same as trading based on your emotions. It usually fails. Basically, there're three reasons why you should exit a trade, namely: when making profits, when losing money, and when you are not making or losing money.

Let us take a brief look at each of these reasons for exiting a trade.

Taking Your Profits

Before you enter a trade, it is important to set a mechanism that tells you it is time to take your profits and exit the trade. Do not rely on some abstract feelings. Remember to be emotionally detached from your trade outcomes.

That way, you will pay more attention to your formerly set mechanism when it alerts you of an exit point. If you are greedy and wait too long, you may lose a substantial part of your profits and if you are too fearful and quit too soon, you may equally lose a significant part of profits that should be yours. This boils down to emotional intelligence.

The good news is that it can be developed. So, if you intend to become a successful swing trader and you have determined that you do not have enough discipline to follow through with your plan, do not worry. You can learn how to do that as you take baby steps in options trading.

When you buy or sell a stock, ensure that you have a stop-loss point in mind. You can use that point to set a stop-loss order, or you can click buy or sell when prices get to that point.

Ending Your Losses

Make up your mind long before you enter any trade that you are going to cut your losses early enough before it digs a hole in your account that will require a lot of money to mend. Again, you must set up a prior mechanism for identifying when to cut your losses. I strongly suggest that you use the trailing stops to cut losses. Set your losses to somewhere around 3% (or less) of your capital. Make your losses as small as possible so you don't get all emotional about the loss.

Be on the lookout for repeated price attempts to breach support or resistance. That is an indication of a possible breakout. Sticking to a losing position in the hope of it rebounding is abandoning your plans and listening to your emotions. In options trading, hope doesn't give you profits. Most often than not, hope has an ironic way of crippling your account.

Freeing Up Your Capital

Whether you choose to quickly exit a trade that is neither making you money nor making you lose money, or you choose to watch it for a few days, both choices are okay. The important thing is that before you enter the trade, you should make up your mind about how long you are willing to watch a trade that is generally lukewarm.

Remember that you are in a type of trade that is considered short-term. You don't have the whole month to wait for one position. If it is tying down your money, free up your capital and reinvest it in another stock or position.

Trading Pullbacks and Rallies

Usually, when stock prices begin to move upward (an uptrend), they tend to pull back briefly. This presents you a good opportunity to buy at low risk and increases your chances of selling at a higher price later. On the reverse side, when stock prices begin to move in a downward direction (downtrend), they tend to rally briefly and offer you an excellent opportunity for shorting.

Here's something for you to consider as a beginner in options trading. If all you do is simply stay in cash (that is, holding on to your money without trading) until you find excellent pullbacks and rallies, you will be making a wise beginner decision.

Think about it. It is known that one of the best times to buy stocks at a great price is right after a recent occurrence of selling. It equally shows better judgment to short sell right after the occurrence of buying.

The best time to trade pullbacks and rallies is the first time they appear on a chart after a significant trend. So, the first time you notice a pullback after a trend line is breached or broken, seize the opportunity.

Buy or sell at that point. When you see a breakout, be ready to trade the first pullback after it. When a new high is set, wait for the first pullback. When it comes up, go in for the kill.

Let us look at the chart below to get a clearer picture of the above. The first pullback after a significant downtrend offered those who were watchful an excellent opportunity to buy early.

You Cannot Win All Trades

No, you can't. It doesn't matter what tools or magic formula you use. Remember that the stock market contains so many moving parts that are far beyond the control of anyone individual or a body. Any of these moving parts could have a significant adverse effect on even the best technical indicators or analysis tools.

But you can win a lot of trades enough to make you good profits. The profits you make come from the ignorance or mistakes of other traders. In the stock market, you are either making mistakes or you are making profits. Unfortunately, for most traders, they are making mistakes. Whether you will choose to make profits depends largely on if you will take your learning seriously to avoid the mistakes most novices make.

Some of these mistakes are depending 100% on technical analysis, being too afraid to lose, looking for a fail-proof system or trading magic formula, being emotional, etc. Not really everyone is cut out to be a trader or a swing trader. However, a lot of people will give it a shot and eventually fail. From these failed attempts, you will make profits if you learn and apply what these other traders won't.

Chapter 6: Risk Management

When you are trading in options, managing your risk in the right way is essential to keep your capital safe. In certain forms of investments, you will come across a situation where exposure to risk is totally unavoidable, and at that time, you have to remind yourself that it is not the exposure to risk that poses the problem but the poor management of risk. Risks will always be there but what you need to keep in mind is that you are not incurring unsustainable losses.

I will introduce you to various ways in which you can manage your risk and also bring home good profits.

Practice Optimal Position Sizing

Position sizing is the first step to effective risk management. Managing risk and managing money are two things that are very closely related to each other. Remember that the amount of money you have in hand is limited, and so, keep track of your budget is vital so that you don't end up losing all your capital. When you learn the concept of position sizing, managing your money becomes easier. The term basically refers to the amount of capital that a trader is using to enter any specific position in the market. Most beginner traders think that position sizing does not require any special planning and can be done randomly, but that is not how it works.

They often think that if they are really confident about a trade, then they can choose a larger position size, and if they are a bit less confident, then a small position size would be apt. But this is not at all a strategic way to approach it.

So, the most effective way of determining the position size is first to figure out how much capital you want to invest in each trade, and then you also need to find out how much that capital is in terms of percentage of your total capital. If you think about it carefully, you will realize that position sizing is not that much different from the concept of diversification. The idea is to allow only a very small percentage of your capital to any single trade, and by doing this, you are risking only a very specific small amount of money. The key aspect here is to ensure that one bad trade does not affect your total capital.

Let us say almost 50% of your total capital has been put into one single trade, and then, you end up losing that trade, then in just one trade, a significant portion of your capital is lost. That is why it is said that you should risk only 1% of your total capital in one trade. This will ensure that even if you had a number of consecutive losses, your overall capital is not affected.

Never Risk More Than You Can Afford to Lose

The consequences of losing the entire capital or most parts of your capital are quite bad. Your aim should be keeping the risk really low, and so, you should not use that much, which you cannot afford to lose. Make a monthly budget and find out what your monthly expenses are. Then keep some money aside for your retirement plan, and then you can set aside money for trading capital. Never use the money for monthly expenses into trading. Similarly, you should not invest your entire trading capital in a single trade.

Stick to Your Trading Plan

It might sound simple to you know how it is a big task to stick to the trading plan, but it is a big task. Some people lose sight of the fact while trading and deviate from the plan. That is when they step into a territory of uncertainty and end up making bad decisions.

Always Have an Exit Plan

One of the important steps of managing risk in options trading is to learn to have an exit plan. There are plenty of variables in this type of trading that you cannot have control over; that is why before you enter a trade, your exit plan should be in place.

Now, what is an exit plan? There are two major things that must be included in an exit plan, and they are:

- If things are not working in your favor, then at what point are you going to get out of the trade?
- If things do work in your favor, then when are you going to take the profits and exit the trade?

Now, if the market conditions don't work out and options become extremely volatile, then you should have a fixed percentage of fluctuation that you would tolerate before getting out of the trade. If 30-50% of the capital invested is already lost, it is time for you to exit the trade before you lose everything. Swallow the losses, learn from your mistakes, and start afresh.

But if things do work out in your favor, then your aim would be to keep your profits safe. The take profit point is a tricky thing, and it usually differs depending on the market condition. You will learn to set this with more precision as you gain more experience in the market.

Every trader spends a lot of time devising their entry strategies, and they forget that if they do not exit the market at the right time, then all their profits would be lost. But an experienced trader always has an exit strategy ready. Even if your entry into the trade was terrible, if you exit it in the right manner, you can be saved. But if your entry was perfect and your exit was wrong, then it can do more harm than good. Also, another thing to keep in mind is figuring out what your maximum potential losses are.

Be Smart While Using Options Spreads

These are some of the most powerful tools you have in the realm of options trading, so you know that these strategies involve the usage of more than one position on options contracts where the underlying stock or asset remains the same.

The spreads are very special because they give you an effective chance to manage your risk. When you are entering a position, you can significantly reduce your upfront costs with the help of these spreads. Also, you can reduce the amount of money you stand to lose in a trade with the help of spreads. The bull call spread is a perfect example of that. In this strategy, your potential for profit does reduce a bit, but in doing so, you are also minimizing your overall risk.

If you want to enter a short position, even then, the proper use of spreads can minimize the risk involved. In both cases, you will be entering the positions with the aim that even if the prices don't go as planned, you still stand to gain some money. This is why spreads are considered to be an excellent strategy for risk management and are used by most options traders. They can also be used in pretty much every market condition.

Diversify

You must have heard of diversification as a risk management strategy whenever we talk about the stock market and mostly when people are into the buy and hold strategy. The basic idea of diversification is that you spread your investments over a wide range of companies and sectors so that you don't have a lot of money tied to any company or sector. But what about options trading? Diversification does not work in the same way here, but you cannot deny the different risk management benefits it has.

In options trading, you can engage in diversification by trading in options that have different types of underlying assets. The ultimate idea remains the same—you are not relying on any single type of security for your profits but diversifying your trades. But this was only one way of diversification, that is, across products.

You can also diversify your trades based on direction. This means you have to ensure that your directional risk has not accumulated on one side. You should have some neutral trades, some bearish trades, and some bullish trades. And lastly, you should also diversify by time. The expiration cycles of your options should be different. This will ensure that their volatility and changes in stock prices are different.

Cover Short Options Soon

Traders often make the mistake of waiting for a long period of time before they can buy back their short options, but you always need to be ready and attentive about them. It is quite natural for you to think that since the trade is going the way you wanted, you can now rest and take a break, but you have to keep in mind that this will not always be the case. Sometimes, trades can quickly start to move in the opposite direction.

If things change all of a sudden and you don't notice, there can be a million excuses for you to give, but nothing will get you back your lost profits.

So, if you notice that your short option is going too much out-of-the-money, then don't think twice before buying it back. Do it now and reduce the risk from your plate. If you are thinking about the profits, then here is something that you should follow—if about 80% or more of your initial profit from the sale of the option stays with you, then don't worry, and buy the option now. Otherwise, if you wait too long, the same short option might come back and be a headache for you.

Chapter 7: The Greeks

One of the things you need to learn about and be aware of when it comes to options trading is the "Greeks." These are parameters with Greek letters that will help you estimate the future behavior of options pricing. So, you need to keep them in mind when considering getting into a trade and exiting your trades. There are five of these parameters in total. They are delta, theta, gamma, rho, and Vega. In most cases, delta and theta are what you need to pay attention to, and the rest are details. As we will see, in today's environment where interest rates are low and not changing by very much, rho isn't of much relevance. But, of course, you should be aware of what rho means because, at some point in the future, interest rates may rise higher or become more volatile.

Vega has some relevance in relation to the volatility of a stock. Most of the time, it's not that important, but as we'll see, there are certain situations when it can impact options prices significantly, and there are strategies that you can use to profit from this.

For the most part, options traders need to be focused on delta and theta. Understanding these two parameters can help you be more aware and effective in your options trading. They will help you to be more informed when it comes to the prospects of a given options contract, and where it is going once you've invested in it. A more informed trader is always going to be a more successful trader, and those who do their trading on the fly are usually the same people that end up with heavy losses.

Delta

The first Greek that we are going to look at is one of the most important. The main piece of information that you are going to get from the delta is the amount that the price of an option is going to change in reaction to the given change of the underlying stock's price. Delta is expressed as a fraction, so it can be viewed as giving you the percentage by which the price of the option will change as a fraction of the change in the stock price. Or you can just look at it in terms of change by a dollar in the stock's price.

Looking at a $235 strike call option on Apple, the delta is 0.5427. So that means there is going to be about a 54 cent change in the price of the option for every dollar price change in Apple stock. You will recall that earlier; we mentioned that there is a rule of thumb for an at-the-money option—it will change by 50 cents for every dollar change in the price of the underlying stock. This proves the point that the option is about $1 in the money, which is barely in the money—and it's going to change by 54 cents, which is quite close to the 50 cent value.

Delta is not a fixed value. You will see it change in real-time as the stock price moves up and down. Of course, in most circumstances, the delta is not going to change very much over a relatively short time period, like a day or so. But you need to be aware that when you go look up the delta and see that it is a specific value, that value is dynamic and not fixed, so you need to keep your eye on how it's changing.

Theta

The second Greek that you want to pay close attention to is called theta. This gives you a relatively precise estimate of the time decay of the option. Theta is expressed as a negative value, which is an indication that it will decrease in value for each passing day. Theta is dynamic like delta, but it will be changing by small amounts in the entire day of trading as long as there is a change in the value of the price of the stock. The main point at which theta becomes important is with turnover. That is, options prices drop at market open due to value lost through time decay. And guess how much they drop? Take theta and multiply it by 100. So, if theta is -0.11, that means that the price of the option is going to automatically drop by $11 when the market opens the next day.

Theta is going to have higher values, the closer the option is to be at the money. Theta has smaller values when options are more in the money, but it also has smaller values when options are more out of the money.

But rather than worrying about the variation, you need to be aware of the value of the theta for any option that you invest in. This way, you can consider the amount of money you are going to lose if you hold any option overnight.

This will have to be considered along with many other factors, of course. But, in some cases, it is not going to be worth it to hold the option overnight and take the hit to the options price. If you have an option that is trading at $100, a theta value of -0.11 means that your option is going to lose 11% of its value overnight. Is that significant? It depends since a movement in share price can easily overwhelm that value. If you were trading call options, and the share price was to go up by 50 cents, with delta equal to say 0.65 that would indicate that the option's price would go up by $32.50 from the delta but drop by $11 from the theta. So, on the net, you'd be profiting. That means both values need to be considered, and you need to be on top of things as far as estimating how the stock is going to move.

Earlier, we mentioned that beginning options traders often make the mistake of holding losing trades all the way through expiration, and they end up losing their entire investment when they could have cut their losses. But there is another problem many beginning traders run into—and that is getting out too early when they should not do so. The above example might illustrate this, believe it or not, many new options traders will panic at the thought of time decay and sell their option before market close, and then the following morning even though the option starts out of the gate taking a hit because of the time decay-driven losses, it quickly recovers and becomes profitable due to a move in the underlying stock price.

Vega

The underlying volatility of a stock is an important factor influencing options prices. Volatility is a measure of how drastically stock prices are changing with time. If a stock has a median share price of $32, and it fluctuates between $30 and $34 over the course of a week, it is far less volatile than a stock that has a median share price of $32, but the second stock fluctuates between $25 and $50 over the same time period. So, volatility is a measure of how much change there is in a share price and how frequently it's changing. You can think of this in terms of graphics as well. A very jagged curve fluctuating up and down between wildly different values is very volatile, while a stable stock price that is practically a smooth line over the same time period is not very volatile.

One measure you can look for on your brokerage account or stock market sites is to look up the value of beta for a given company. Beta is a comparison of the stock's volatility relative to the market average. It is expressed as being greater or less than 1. The stock market average is normalized to 1.0. Any value greater than 1.0 indicates a highly volatile stock, while a value of less than 1.0 indicates a stock that is not very volatile.

If you look up a given stock, and you find that beta is 1.53 that means it's 53% more volatile than the market average. On the other hand, if you look up a stock and find that beta is 0.4, that means it's only 40% as volatile as the average. Beta is actually calculated using five-year averages.

The volatility of a stock really doesn't have anything to do with whether or not the stock is desirable to own as an investment. Some very highly desirable stocks have high beta values, but some have relatively low beta values.

Gamma

Gamma is one of the Greeks that get less attention, and it's a little more complicated, which might be one of the reasons that it's not tops on most people's lists. The value of paying much attention to it is not as clear cut either. Gamma is a quantity that gives you the rate of change of delta. It will tell you the amount of change in the value of delta you can expect when the stock price changes. Gamma values tend to be pretty small, on the order of 0.01-0.03 or so. For example, let the share price be $100, delta 0.65, and gamma 0.01. If the share price were to rise $1 that would mean that delta would rise to 0.66. If gamma had been 0.03, then the value of delta would have changed to 0.68 for the same $1 change in the share price.

Rho

The last of the Greeks is rho. We are leaving that to the end because these days, Rho is the least important of the Greeks. Rho is related to interest rates. Specifically, the value of rho is related to a hypothetical "risk-free" interest rate. It gives you an estimate of how the option's price would change relative to a one-point change in the risk-free interest rate. Since interest rates are not changing by large amounts in today's environment, this is not going to be a quantity that is going to require much attention.

So, what is the risk-free interest rate? This is an estimate of what the interest rate would be if you had your money in a risk-free investment. Interest rates for the past ten years have been at historic lows. Generally, the risk-free interest rate is taken to be the interest rate on a 10-year U.S. Treasury. That is about as close as you can get to a risk-free investment. You are pretty much guaranteed, at least for the time being, of getting your capital back if you invest in ten year U.S. government bonds.

Chapter 8: Algorithmic Trading

What is an Algorithm?

" **A**n algorithm is a set of unambiguous instructions for performing a task. Algorithms can execute automatically (as in a computer program) or manually (as in an unautomated process). An algorithm has inputs and outputs. "

The term "algorithm" is derived from the name of Persian mathematician Abū Ja'far Muhammad ibn Mūsā al-Khwārizmī, often Latinized as "Algoritmi" and called "the father of algorithmic art". He wrote several treatises on the Hindu-Arabic numeral system in the 9th century, but most of them have not survived.

What is Algorithmic Trading?

Algorithmic trading is a method of executing a large order (too large to fill all at once) using automated pre-programmed trading instructions accounting for variables such as time, price, and volume to send small slices of the order (child orders) out to the market over time.

Algorithmic Trading is the set of rules and procedures used by investors or their advisors to issue orders automatically based on certain pre-defined parameters.

Why Use Algorithmic Trading?

The idea behind algorithmic trading is to use advanced computer algorithms to reduce human irrationality and emotions. The benefits of automated trading are numerous and include:

- Reduction in trading costs - by placing many orders at once, the market impact cost of each individual trade is significantly decreased.

- Reduction in Capital Requirements - by executing a large order over time, you can often invest more with less capital.

- More flexibility - since algorithmic traders are not bound to pre-determined schedules, they can execute trades based on immediate market conditions. This provides investors with improved liquidity and the ability to respond quickly to changing markets.

Algorithmic trading systems are used in every major financial market around the world, including stocks, futures, foreign exchange (forex), options, bonds, and commodities.

Working of Algorithmic Trading System:

The algorithmic trading system works on a mathematical algorithm based on the commonly available market data. The algorithmic trading system is a set of rules that are fully automated by the computer-based program. It means no human involvement in the whole trading process. The software monitors the market continuously and makes automated decisions about when to buy or sell shares or other financial instruments.

An algorithmic trading systems program sets the rules and monitors the market for opportunities to take advantage of. It can place bids and offers on your behalf in a fast and efficient manner.

How Algorithmic Trading System Works?

The algorithmic trading system works on a mathematical algorithm based on the commonly available market data. The traders set the mathematical equations before they are fed into a computer, which then decides when to buy or sell shares or other financial instruments on their behalf based on pre-programmed instructions.

The trader may define simple entry and exit rules or more complex pricing models to execute the trades.

Algo Trading can be done in one of two ways: direct or indirect.

Note: The Methods used for Algorithmic Trading may be either Manual or Semi-Automatic, where the trader makes the decision and then the computer executes the trade, however, in a fully automated system such as ADL (Automated Delivery of Liquidity) by Comex, there is no human intervention at all. In an ADL system, a client can simply connect their trading platform to that of Comex and allow their orders to be automatically executed by the ADL system with no intervention on their part whatsoever.

The indirect method uses the data feeds from stock exchanges to find out the real-time value of the shares. Based on this information and by using specific pre-programmed rules, an algorithm can then decide when to buy or sell shares. This is basically how all online brokers operate.

The direct method involves two parts: The first is the monitoring of data feeds from stock exchanges and other sources of information, and an algorithm analyzing this data to decide whether to buy or sell shares based on pre-defined instructions. The second part is a direct connection with the stock exchange through a dedicated line (leased line) where child orders are sent directly to the exchange without passing through an online broker's computer system. This method is slower than the indirect method because it involves the transmission of orders through a leased line and the response for execution is received after a small delay. However, some firms use this method as they are worried about their online brokers using their algorithms and information to trade against them.

How to Start Algo Trading?

It's not easy to start algorithmic trading. It involves purchasing some software and hiring some people with the necessary skills. However, one can outsource it if he wants to do algorithmic trading on a small scale. Some financial service companies, for example, sell pre-programmed trading algorithms (generally called "systems") that investors can use with their own money. Most of these systems can be used to trade a variety of assets, including stocks, options and futures. Some systems trade only one asset such as gold or silver.

However, not all algorithmic trading is done by big institutions with teams of people and lots of capital. Non-professional algorithmic traders are generally known as "retail algorithmic traders" because they use their own money to fund their trading operations. These individual investors often enter trades manually, but use algorithmic trading software for "dealing" with the execution of specific trades, such as placing orders on the buy and sell sides simultaneously in order to capture the spread.

Other than that, in order to automate your algorithmic trading system; you need the following:

1. An Internet connection
2. A trading platform (this can be an individual software or a service that can connect you with the financial exchanges)
3. An Algorithm (this is basically a set of instructions that tell your computer when to buy or sell shares or other financial instruments).
4. Financial Market Data (to see how the market is performing and where there may be opportunities to trade)
5. A Broker (to execute trades with your broker and provide you with market data)

6. Risk Management and Money management (This is basically the backtesting part of it. Backtesting involves running a simulation on historical data to see how profitable your algorithm could have been).

Pros and Cons of Algorithmic Trading

There are both pros and cons in algorithmic trading. Here are some of them:

Benefits: Algorithmic trading is very advantageous because it can be done 24 hours a day, 365 days a year without requiring any human intervention.

It is generally faster than a manual trader, and more reliable since it performs error checks and can recover from system failure or other interruptions to a trading session.

It is cost effective in terms of labor cost. A computer doesn't get tired of doing the same job for hours on end, a human being does. This means that it's cheaper to pay a computer to trade for you all day long rather than paying an employee that will get tired doing it.

Algorithmic trading requires lower investment capital as compared to human discretionary traders.

Drawbacks: The software that comes with algorithmic trading may not be perfect and can make mistakes resulting in losses in the portfolio.

It is important to note that the Algo Trading Software may not be able to handle large market movements and an unexpected crash in the market can result in a devastating loss for the trader.

Since algorithmic trading uses logic to make decisions based on prices, there is no room for emotions which could result in poor decision-making.

Despite this, as an individual trader using these methods, I find them very useful because they allow me to see opportunities I wouldn't have noticed otherwise or perform analysis on my trade ideas very quickly. That way, you get all the advantages of automated trading without any of its drawbacks.

Chapter 9: Habits and Mindset of the Financially Free

In this topic, we will focus on mindset and how it impacts options trading both positively and negatively. First, it is very important to understand what mindset is and the types in case of any. Therefore, Mindset refers to the assumptions, notions, and beliefs that a person has or how they view incidents and interpret them.

Mindsets exist in two different forms, that is, a growth mindset and a fixed mindset. A fixed mindset is where a person will always have certain thoughts and views towards something, and in case of problems, they believe they can find a solution to them. A growth mindset is that one will view life or any situation from different angles and points of view. To them, they would always find solutions to problems by all means. People with a growth mindset tend to act with enthusiasm and are always willing to learn or develop new skills to help them find solutions. Those with fixed mindsets usually do not grow mentally and in other spheres as they fix themselves to certain life positions without any intent to change.

The Mindset in Options trading

Before venturing into options trading, the kind of mindset that you have towards it is very vital. This is because the sale and purchase of securities need to be thought about carefully least one makes losses rather than profits. Apart from that, options trading for a long time has become a hard nut to crack too many as they believe that it is a very hard investment. With this kind of mindset, it would be hard for someone to overcome the various hurdles associated with this investment. When faced with problems, one can even quit if they have a fixed mindset or make poor decisions that will sire consecutive losses in the long run.

This, therefore, means that there is a strong relationship between one's mindset and trading options. This is because the mindset is the one that can either determine losses or profits. The following are some instances where the mindset is related to options trading:

Decision Making

Like any other kind of investment, options trading also has a series of situations that require one to make vital decisions that will decide the future of the investment. When buying or selling options (securities), the price is usually determined for a certain period. When buying options, one always has to decide what will allow them to make a profit when they decide to sell in the future. On the first go, one might unexpectedly go on a loss if the decision was not so good. This makes many lose hope and have the mindset that options trading is a complicated investment, which is not the case.

A person who has a fixed mindset will always view options trading to be complicated and very hard to venture into. With this mindset, it would be very hard for them to make a sane decision at any given point. This may cost them by making the run into consecutive losses to the point of quitting options trading.

On the other hand, a person who has a growth mindset will try to look for solutions for the problem and how they can go about it to make profits once again.

This is a person who will learn from the first poor decision and focus on making a better decision the next time they trade. This person, with time, will have learned all the required skills to trade and make profits. This, therefore, proves to us that mindset has got a very strong link to options trading.

Risk-Taking

Every investment is characterized by various risks that are associated with it. Options trading is not an exception, as it also has many risks capable of negatively impacting the investment. One of the major risks is making losses and getting major disappointments. Another risk is being bankrupt, which is a result of the chain of losses. Despite all these risks that endanger your investment's sustenance, the mindset you have will always determine whether it will succeed or fall.

A person with a fixed mindset in this kind of situation might easily give up. This is because the individual will view options trading as a losing investment that does them no good. It would be even more dangerous if one continues trading with this kind of mindset. This is because they would never expect anything less than losses. On the other hand, a person with a growth mindset will take the loss as a steppingstone. They would then use these instances to develop new approaches and skills that will help them overcome this risk. In the end, this person will make profits and enjoy the investment as he will be well equipped with the necessary skills for risk management.

Flexibility

In options trading, one is supposed to always be flexible, just like any other kind of investment out there. Options trading has got different terms and conditions that possibly change over time. Before making a sale or purchase of options, one should be well conversant and equipped with the trade knowledge. Failure to abide by these conditions might find your trade obsolete and might lead you to losses. Some of these terms and conditions are usually harsh and very hard to abide by them, thus requiring you to change the trading approach you use to remain valid. Having the right mindset is also vital in strictly ensuring that your trade is in line with the set conditions.

If you have negative reasoning and a fixed mindset towards the set conditions and terms, you might not succeed in the trade. You will tend to focus on the negatives that they are doing to the trade rather than positively impact it. This will, therefore, make you drift focus from making profits through options sales and purchases to change in the conditions. This will thus guarantee you a series of losses in the investment. On the other hand, for a person who has a positive and growth mindset, the change of the terms and conditions will be a non-issue to them. This is because they will easily devise new trading approaches that will fit the conditions and continue making profits. This thus depicts a great relation between the mindset of a person and options trading.

Does Mindset Matter in Options Trading?

If we are not dealing with investments, such as options trading, there are several challenges we face in the development of our activities. These challenges are faced by everyone, and some will comfortably overcome them while some will just whine and cry over them without looking for any possible solutions. This all depends on the person's mindset, either a growth mindset or a fixed mindset. A fixed mindset will give up on life and make no step in trying to count these problems. On the other hand, an individual with a growth mindset will think over the problem and develop a solution using their skills to overcome this problem.

In terms of investments and options trading, nothing is different, as the same also applies. Having a fixed mindset makes you only cry over problems you face in the trade rather than come up with solutions. Therefore, it is clear that someone who has a growth mindset will definitely do better in trading compared to the one with a fixed mindset. Individuals with fixed mindsets are always said to seem to seek approval. They will even try to prove themselves in the trading and fail to look for more information as they might be wrong. In any situation, there is always the call for confirming their intelligence, character, or personality. They also evaluate situations that they are in to determine if they will succeed or not.

Having a growth mindset usually leads to the quest for more knowledge and the desire to make discoveries and work hard. Apart from that and most importantly, having a growth mindset will make one tackle challenges, thus grow in all spheres of life comfortably. Individuals with a growth mindset will fail when they try as a learning experience, which will eventually lead them to change, growth, and success. When it comes to options trading, they will not see losses they make as disappointments or losing it in life generally. Instead, they will see it as a challenge and opportunity to grow and put in place strategies that will help solve the issue. With this spirit, it would be very easy to conduct options trading and make very big profits. From this, we can, therefore, come up with a conclusion that mindset is very critical in options trading. It may determine whether you are going to make a profit from your trade or losses. It also depicts the resilience level you have that will enable you to keep up the options trading despite any problems that might come your way. Apart from that, mindset matters because it will depict the future of your options trade. It will determine if it will grow and be better or worst. This, therefore, calls for every individual who does options trading to have the right mindset, and they will be able to do well in it.

Traits of an Individual with the Right Mindset in Options Trading

Having the right mindset in options trading is something that one expresses how they do their trading activities. In the current financial markets, options are very versatile and vital instruments. For an individual to trade in these options, they should have the right mindset to succeed in the long last. This, therefore, means that they should possess certain personality traits. These traits include:

Patience

Patience is one of the qualities that options traders possess. Patient investors will always be willing and ready to wait until the market provides the right chances and opportunities. This is opposed to always trying to reap big profits from every movement in the market. Therefore, traders will always be seen as idle while they are busy keeping an eye on the market waiting for a perfect time to exit or enter a trade. Other traders who might be armatures or generally not serious with the trade would quickly do trades, and due to their impatience, they will easily exit or enter trades. An individual with the right mindset in options trading should also be patient.

Discipline

To be a successful options trader, one should be much disciplined. Many activities in options trading, such as looking for opportunities, forming strategies, adhering to them, and even venturing into the right trade, require much discipline. A common example of indiscipline that happens too many is doing as others do. An opinion given by someone else is never trustworthy since they might have researched from a different point of view compared to yours. This might lead to losses that you cannot blame them for it.

Chapter 10: Trading Options to Gain Financial Freedom

T rading options have the great potential to be a form of passive income. This is the complete opposite of active income, which is what most people engage in. Active income is one where a person invests time in exchange for money.

Passive income allows you to enjoy your time still as you dictate while earning money. It comes to you on automatic even while you sleep. While it usually takes time, effort, and maybe monetary input initially, over the long-term, if done right, you can sustain the lifestyle you want if you put forth that investment now.

Passive Income:

- Gives you the platform to gain financial stability, security, and independence.
- Gives you the freedom to do whatever you wish with your time without the worry of sustaining your financial life.
- Gives you the freedom to pursue the career, hobbies, and other activities you love and enjoy rather than having to trade your time for money.
- Allows you to secure your financial future, thus getting rid of your worry, stress, and anxiety in that department.

- Gives you the flexibility to live and work from anywhere in the world, typically. The bonus of this means you get to travel if that is a pursuit you would like to take on while still earning.

Trading options can give you the benefits listed above and thus, light the way to your financial freedom.

My goal when writing this book was to show you how you can take control of your finances, pay off your debt, and live life on your terms using one powerful strategy.

As I mentioned above, having a growth mindset means that you openly receive information from other people to better yourself and your financial life. I share my knowledge with you in this insightful guide because I have implemented these same strategies with tremendous success. It is not a perfect system but it works well if done right and consistently.

Before I invite you to delve in, let me say this... To gain the most benefit from reading the information to come, you need to cultivate the growth mindset mentioned above. You have to also treat this like a business, not a side gig. This is not a hobby nor something that you are just dabbling in. Make an effort and time you invest count. Make it consistent and be persistent. Set a schedule and work on this every day. Make goals for yourself and give yourself a timeline for your accomplishments. Stay focused and committed.

The world's wealth is majorly divided into a small part of the population. Only a small percentage has financial freedom. You can put yourself and your family in that small percentile using this method for passive income. I have faith that you can do it as long as you put in that initial effort. The question is—do you believe that you can do too? Can you envision yourself as the person who has attained financial freedom in the future and is living the life you want?

Answer YES to both these questions and believe in that answer, I implore you!

Now, without further ado, let's jump into this invaluable guide so that you can start the future you desire today.

Chapter 11: Starter Options Trading Strategies

While the early days of your options trading career are likely to consist of a persistent feeling of information overload, there are certain areas where you don't have to worry about learning too much from scratch too soon. Specifically, there are numerous different basic strategies that you can use as a way of focusing on the types of skills you are learning in a productive direction. When it comes to planning out your ultimate success rates, it is essential to keep in mind that while the following strategies are certainly going to help you improve your overall success rate, it is still never going to be a sure thing. No matter how good at trading options you are, losing out on a trade that appeared to be a sure thing will always be a part of the process.

The Buy-Write

This strategy is also known as a covered call. It is ideal if you are unsure about a specific underlying stock because it lets you buy in with confidence regardless of the current market conditions. How it works is that after you purchase the underlying stock in question, you go ahead and create a call that is set to the number of the underlying shares of stock that you now own. This is an excellent options if you will be otherwise occupied shortly and don't want to worry about the underlying stock as you know that you will still be seeing the benefits of premiums if nothing else. It will also help you protect investments that were made on a longer time frame as you will know that you will hold onto a profitable sale price if nothing else. This strategy can be especially useful when paired with LEAPS, funds that were purchased via a margin and index futures, and traditional stocks.

For example, to use this strategy successfully, you would start by purchasing a single options in a given underlying stock, costing you $38 and then selling it at $48. Meanwhile, you would pay $1 for the call and then be able to go about your business knowing that you were going to make $100 even if the market doesn't move. This, in turn, drives each share's cost up to about $47, which means that if the stock drops a second time, the shares will stay where they are at, which means your $100 premium is entirely secure.

Great Combination

Also known as the synthetic long stock strategy, the long combination is utilized by purchasing a call and putting the same details at the same strike price. You will want the underlying asset price to be quite close to the strike price when you pull the trigger. This is a bullish strategy, and the short put is uncovered, which leaves you with a significant amount of risk if things go wrong. As such, this strategy is only recommended when the indicators you favor show that the market is likely to move in the way you expect.

This strategy is known as the long synthetic stock because the risk and reward are nearly the same as the more common long stock strategy. Additionally, if you hold onto the position until it expires, you will likely end up purchasing the underlying asset anyway. Specifically, if the underlying asset ends up higher than the strike price, then you will want to exercise the call. Meanwhile, if it is below the strike price, the put will likely be assigned, which means you will still need to purchase the asset.

With that being said, there is no limit to how much you want the underlying asset to move once you have set up this strategy, the more positive momentum it has, the more money you stand to make. The maximum amount you can expect to lose if things don't go according to plan is limited to the amount of the strike price plus the net debit or minus the net credit.

In this case, purchasing the call will give you the right to buy the underlying asset at the strike price. Selling the put at the same rate then obligates you to buy the underlying asset at this price if you find yourself in a situation where the options is assigned.

Risk Reversal

This is a hedging strategy that involves selling a call and buying a put options. This then mitigates the risk of downward price movements that are unfavorable while limiting the total potential for profit from any upward changes. If you are trading in the forex market, then the risk reversal is the difference in volatility between the put and the call.

If you are short on an underlying instrument, then hedging with this position involves implementing a long risk reversal via the purchase of a call options. You would then write a put options on the same underlying asset. On the other hand, if you are long on an underlying asset, you would short the risk reversal to hedge the position via the writing of a call and purchasing a put options related to the same underlying asset.

Fibonacci Strategy

To utilize this strategy, you can use any chart that you see fit as long as it contains either a run-up or a run down in price and multiple retracements. Next, all you need to do is to begin drawing Fibonacci lines on the chart. If you draw Fibonacci lines on a steady downtrend, you will want to start from the high point on the table and then move towards the lowest swing point. Otherwise, the inverse is true. With this done all you need to do is determine the confluence points that can come from any Fibonacci level, be it 38%, 50%, 62% or 79%.

To use Fibonacci extensions with this strategy, the basics are going to be mostly the same. You will only choose a chart that catches your eye and then add in Fibonacci lines, except this time, you will want Fibonacci extensions enabled as well. You will then look for the confluence points where the ranges overlap to determine what a likely entry point is going to be.

Fibonacci numbers are exceedingly useful as they naturally reflect the psychology of the traders in the market. One of the most valuable times to utilize Fibonacci levels is when it comes to determining the resistance and support of markets that are currently ranging. It doesn't matter if it is long or short; a range will eventually break because an exchange cannot stay in an indecisive position forever.

To determine how a ranging or sideways market will break, all you need to do is specify the range on the timeframe you prefer and then determine the low and the high of that range. If the Fibonacci levels indicated that the price will break above the range, then an uptrend is likely to form, and if it breaks below the range, then a downtrend is expected to develop.

Call First Spread

The call front spread strategy allows you to purchase a call at the money or slightly below the funds at a discounted price compared to purchasing the options on its own. Furthermore, the ultimate goal is to gain the call at the first strike price for credit or only a small debit by selling a pair of calls at the second-strike price. Both strike prices will use the same month of expiration.

It is essential to keep in mind that there is a massive ceiling for risk in this scenario. If the underlying stock moves more than you have anticipated by a significant margin nothing is protecting your real interests. As such, you should only try this strategy if you feel only a little bullish as you want the underlying stock to move to the second-strike price but then stop altogether. If you are not quite sure what the strength of the market will be, the skip strike butterfly call is more appropriate.

For the best results, you will want to see the underlying stock price raise a small amount from the first strike price to the second. This will cover one of the calls that you sold while leaving the second one open to generate more reward or risk if things do not work out in your favor. It is essential to keep a close eye on the underlying stock to ensure that unexpected moves aren't quickly countered and by having an ironclad stop loss in place, just in case. This risk can further be mitigated by using index options instead of traditional options because indexes are even less volatile than individual underlying stocks with low volatility. After all, various price movements tend to cancel out significant movement in either direction.

Straddle

The straddle can be used to either go long or short. The long straddle can be extremely useful if you feel as though the price of a given underlying asset is going to move significantly in one direction, you don't know what direction that will ultimately be. To utilize this strategy, you will need to purchase a put and a call, both using the same underlying asset, strike price, and timeframe. After the long straddle has been created successfully, you will be guaranteed to generate a profit if the amount in question moves in either direction before it expires.

On the other hand, if you are interested in utilizing a short straddle, you will instead want to sell a call and a put with the same costs, timeframe and underlying asset. This will allow you to profit from the premium, even if everything else doesn't turn out as well as you may have liked. This guaranteed profit means that this is a particularly useful strategy if you don't expect to see movement very much in either direction before the options expires. Nevertheless, it is still important to remember that the chances that this strategy will be successful are directly related to the odds that the underlying asset will move in the first place.

Long Strangle

To make use of a long strangle, you will need to purchase a call and a put that is based on the same underlying asset along with the same maturation level. They will need to have different strike prices, however. The strike price for the call should be above the price for the put, and both should start at a point that is out-of-the-money. This is an especially useful strategy if you expect the underlying asset to move a good deal but are unclear about which direction it will choose. When utilized correctly, you will be practically guaranteed to profit after the related costs have been taken into account.

Chapter 12: Basic Options Trading Strategies

A huge load of investors and merchants lose money in options trading since they exchange options without understanding its perplexing subtleties first.

A solid strategy is required to profit from the exchange. It allows a person to grow the profit and reduce the threat. It requires only a little effort to sort out some way to use the power of options and flexibility.

The Covered Call

The Covered Call strategy allows a theorist to buy the underlying asset completely. By then, the monetary expert ought to create and sell a call options following that comparable asset's purchase. The number of offers should be the same.

Monetary experts use this strategy for their flashing exchange and fair appraisal of the underlying asset. It is also used by those brokers who need to make sure about their theory against any possible reduction in worth. It's a good major strategy in any case, and in case you're worried about missing on a possible endeavor, by then, this is the best methodology.

The Married Put

The Married Put strategy is used when investors are bullish about the price of an underlying asset. They buy segments of the asset without a doubt, and a short time later buys a put options at the same time of a comparative number of offers. They do this to guarantee their endeavor against likely setbacks on a current second. It's a technique to money on a hypothesis at present; anyway, they don't have to worry about losing anything when difficult situations emerge. The potential for gains in this is boundless.

The married put strategy looks like the security that chooses a story price if an enthusiastic one makes a plunge the asset's price.

The Bull Call Spread

The Bull Call Spread strategy is used when investors are bullish over a particular asset, and they foresee the price of the underlying asset rise bearably.

They buy a call options at a particular strike price by simultaneously creating and selling a call options at a more extravagant expense. Exactly when induced, the vendor buys the lower-priced asset, by then at the same time sells the more extreme asset—thus, creating advantage.

For this strategy to work, both call options ought to have a comparable underlying asset and expiration month.

The Bear Put Spread

The Bear Put Spread strategy is used when investors are bearish about the price of an underlying asset. For the present circumstance, they foresee that the price ought to diminish moreover.

They buy a put options at a particular price, by then make and sell one more put options at a price lower than their first options. Exactly when prompted, the dealer sells the more costly asset, by then at the same time re-buys the lower-priced asset like this, creating advantage moreover.

Like the bull call spread, this may be successful if monetary experts execute a comparable asset with practically identical expiration dates. This strategy limits both advantage and, even more essentially, disaster.

The Protective Collar

The Protective Collar strategy ties down advantage without the need to sell the segments of the underlying asset. Monetary investors buy an out-of-the-money put options, by then create and sell an out-of-the-money call options. Again, this conceivably works if monetary experts execute with a comparative asset.

It is used by monetary experts who go long in an underlying asset and have obtained profits. If the asset price drops, the held Put options will ensure advantages. If the asset price rises, you secure an advantage once someone rehearses your formed call options.

The Long Straddle

The Long Straddle strategy is used to confine disasters and care for increments.

For the present circumstance, the mishap is confined unmistakably to the price of the options.

Monetary experts should buy a put and a call options at a comparative price, a comparative expiration date, and an underlying comparative asset to be productive. They use this strategy when they acknowledge that the price of the asset will move drastically. Regardless, they don't know about the bearing the price will take.

The Long Strangle

The Long Strangle (not to be confused with the preceding one) strategy is a more affordable strategy than the long straddle, considering how the options are bought out-of-the-money. It is used to limit disasters to the price of the put and call options. Besides, monetary experts use this strategy to acknowledge that the underlying asset's price will move basically. Nevertheless, they don't realize which bearing the price will move.

To be powerful, examiners buy both a put and a call options with a comparative asset and the same expiry date. Anyway, the prices of the options change from each other. The strike price of the put options should be under the call options strike price. Accordingly, the options will both result in out-of-the-money.

The Butterfly Spread

The Butterfly Spread strategy is a blend of the bear spread and the bull spread strategies. It furthermore uses various prices. Such a butterfly spread strategy grants monetary experts a call options at the most insignificant strike price. They simultaneously form and sell two call options at a more extravagant expense and another call options at the most critical possible price. So, if someone rehearses your created options, you rapidly practice yours. You end up selling high and buying low—subsequently prompting advantage.

Furthermore, it is achievable for them to purchase a put options at the best expense by simultaneously making and selling two put options at a lower strike price while selling the last put options in any event strike price. So, if someone rehearses your made options, you speedily practice yours. You again end up selling high and buying low—therefore inducing advantage again.

The Iron Condor

The Iron Condor strategy is difficult to execute. It's not for new options theorists since it requires a huge load of time and practice to be productive. Monetary experts have both a short and long circumstance in 2 kinds of strangling procedures: a bearish and a bullish course.

However, paying little heed to which course, if someone rehearses your made options, you rapidly practice yours. Done adequately, you end up selling high and buying low—likewise provoking advantage again.

While using this options technique, put forth an attempt not to dumbfound the strike prices. You should reliably end up buying lower and selling higher.

The Iron Butterfly

The Iron Butterfly combines a short or long straddle with a strangle. It is genuinely equal to the butterfly spread. Regardless, what is important is that the iron butterfly uses a put and a call options simultaneously. This strategy limits mishaps and gains inside a particular reach. Monetary experts ensure costs are restricted, and peril is confined by using out-of-the-money options.

The Synthetic Long Call Strategy

This is a strategy used when two procedures for spreading are used with another long call strategy. For example, if you used a married long call with a bear call, this would be a synthetic long call. The purpose behind this is to settle on two long decisions of a comparative sort. It can assist you with procuring pay as time goes on, and there are central focuses to this. One thing to recollect notwithstanding is to guarantee that you're not doing anything unnecessarily dangerous with everything into account. Choose whether the call is advocated, notwithstanding all the difficulty, and subsequently act after that. Understanding what the threats are is how you'll be powerful with the synthetic long call.

Collar Call

A Collar Call is where you use underlying stock along with protective puts and selling call options. You use the puts and the selling call against the underlying stock. The inspiration driving this is because they are out-of-money options, and from this current, it resembles the out-of-money covered call. It is used to get charges on options without taking a risk with the conceivable mishap in the long-term because of the drop of price or the set apart down the security peril.

These options strategies will help you understand where you're going with this and starting there, and you can choose the method of where your approach will go. It's basic to acknowledge where all that will end up falling, considering how numerous events people don't comprehend the genuine quintessence of various calls. Knowing the spreads and potential strategies will help you control the market better achieve better results.

Chapter 13: Advanced Options Trading Strategies

I n options trading there are various strategies, the following are strategies for advanced users:

1. Bull Spread: it is a common strategy taken when the investor expects a price to go up but slow. The investor buys calls and sells calls; therefore, he has to pay only for the long call and receive money for the short call.

2. Bear spread: it is another options trading strategy that is similar to bull spread, but in this case, the investor expects a price to go down, but at a slow pace, then he/she buys puts and sells calls; therefore, they will get money for selling calls and have to pay for buying puts.

3. Butterfly spread: this is a strategy that is considered low-risk and one of the most popular strategies. The investor will buy two options with different strike prices and sell two options with the same strike price. The investor will make an income of the premium value for selling both options and pay only for one options.

4. Iron Condor: like butterfly spread, in this strategy also the investor has to buy two call options whereas he/she sell two

put options, but unlike butterfly spread, in this case, both options have different strike prices.

5. Calendar spread: it is a strategy where the investor will buy an options with more time remaining in the maturity date and sell (write) an options with less time left in the maturity date. The investor has to pay for more time left in the maturity date, however, will receive premium value for having a short position on the other options.

6. Stock swap: this is a strategy that does not involve risk as the investor will simply buy one stock and write one call on another stock of the same company or industry. Here both stocks belong to the same company but they have different strike prices. Thus, the investor will lose if the company stock price goes above or below a certain level.

7. Butterfly: this is an advanced strategy where the investor buys both call and put options on different strike prices and same expiration date however has different strike prices.

8. Calendar: this is an advanced strategy where the investor purchases an options with more time left until maturity date and sells (writes) an options with less time left until maturity date just like calendar spread; here also one has to pay for a long options but receive money for selling a short options.

9. Conversion: it is an advanced strategy where the investor buys a call options and writes a put options for the same

stock and same strike price, the investor will make money if the stock price goes up or down but if it stays stagnant then he/she will lose money.

10. Reverse conversion: the investor will buy put options and writes call options, for the same stock and the same strike price, it is the opposite of conversion strategy and in case if the price stays stagnant or goes down then one will make money.

Chapter 14: Day Trading Strategies

D ay trading is a double-edged sword, you can reap substantial rewards, but you could lose your shirt by betting wrong. But it doesn't have to be an activity that carries huge amounts of risk. By following a few commonsense tips, you can minimize your risks and ensure that your profits are more likely.

Set Aside Capital for Day Trading

Don't be the person that bets the farm on hoping to cash in big. You should set aside capital that you are willing to lose for day trading. More importantly, you should set aside an amount of capital that you can afford to lose so that you're not begging relatives for money to pay your rent if your trades go bad.

Use Stop Losses

Even the most careful day trader can run into trouble. You can minimize your losses by planning ahead of time. Each time you place an order, make sure to use stop losses so that your losses will be minimized if your bet turns out to be wrong.

Do your homework

As they say, knowledge is power. People who fail as day traders buy and sell stocks based on superficial looks at the markets and rely on hunches. Those who make long-term profits are those who carefully study the markets. That means being familiar with the stock market, recent behavior on the stock market, the companies you're looking to trade and the economy at large. Day trading is going to be a full-time activity. You will need to keep up with the economic outlook in the short term. You'll need to know what the Fed is going to be doing with interest rates. You'll have to follow international trade and look for political events that can impact the markets. You will need to read financial websites daily and subscribe to publications like the Wall Street Journal, Bloomberg and the Financial Times. You'll also need to spend time watching CNBC and Fox Business to get the latest news as soon as possible. It's also a good idea to make short lists of companies to study several in detail so that you are acting on good information rather than playing guessing games.

Start Small

When you are learning how to day trade, chances are you're going to have a lot of failures. Therefore, it's best to start with small trades with small amounts of capital and limited numbers of shares. Buying options is a good way to start as well since you can speculate only risking the premiums rather than spending large amounts of money upfront. When you start small, you can gain the necessary experience without losing all your capital first. As you gain experience and confidence you can increase the amount invested.

No Penny Stocks

Stick with stocks on the major stock exchange. Now and then, penny stocks will turn out to be hidden gems, but most of the time there is a reason that they are penny stocks. They are best avoided as they'll be losers most of the time.

Time for Volatility

The first and last hours of the trading day are when many people will be making their moves for the day, either bidding stocks up or frantically selling. The mid-day is going to be a time of lower volatility. When you are first starting, you might want to avoid the first half-hour of trading.

Practice Makes Perfect

Consider doing practice trades for a while, i.e., study the techniques used in day trading and then look at real data in the markets to decide what strategies you'd employ with a given stock, and then follow it without actually making the trade. The point here is to practice without risking capital for a short period so that you can gain some experience before actually trading. There are stock trading simulators you can play with, for example:

- https://ninjatrader.com

- https://tradingsim.com

Don't Get Greedy

Using pivot points is a good strategy. It's going to be tempting to try and wait things out when a stock moves rapidly in the direction you're betting on. But if you wait too long to act, you may end up missing out on profits. Don't get greedy and take what profits you can get using pre-determined limits.

Avoid Being Taken Over by Emotion

This is related to the last point, but it also relates to panic. If you're long on security but it doesn't look good for a while, don't panic and get out too early. This is the converse of being too greedy. It's human nature to panic, but in the stock markets, that's what the amateurs do. Using the pivot point example, you know ahead of time what your limits are. Using limit orders is the best way to avoid panic because you'll have your exit strategy set up already, so it will happen automatically.

Plan Your Trade and Trade Your Plan

The key to succeeding while day trading is to plan. You should already have your strategy mapped out before you move on it. You will have to act fast when the buying or selling condition arrives, but you won't need to think about it or agonize with emotion if you're planned things out ahead of time.

Chapter 15: Trading Analysis

What is Trading Analysis?

T here are many traders out there who believe that you should never go to sleep without having done your research and checked the trading data. This may be done in a variety of ways, but it can be categorized into two main types:

Some people like to trade the currency charts and mainly rely on their instincts for money management issues; they claim that they don't need any technical analysis tools because their eyes give them all the information they need. On the other hand, others believe that charting is just one of a few tools necessary for successful currency trading and that using sentiment and news events and a technique called trading analysis is also crucial for successful trading.

In Options Trading, Trading Analysis is also known as Technical Analysis. The main purpose of technical analysis is to determine the current and future price movement of a security based on its past trading prices. Trading analysis can also be used in equities, futures, commodities, and currencies; it is simply necessary for all types of financial instruments traded on the market.

So, what type of tools does technical analysis use? Well, there are a lot of different techniques and indicators available to the trader. A few of the most common tools include:

Chart Pattern

This is one of the most commonly used technical analysis techniques. When you apply this method, you simply need to look for a chart pattern that may form after the market has experienced a significant move. Three or more points will determine a chart pattern, and you'll need to identify where these points are located on the chart. Once you have identified these points, you'll need to draw lines between them to form your pattern; then, all that is left is to identify whether a new trend will develop based on your pattern. There are a variety of chart patterns that you may encounter.

Spot Technique

A lot of traders like to apply the spot technique when using technical analysis. This is the easiest method to use, and it can be used to pick tops and bottoms in the market.

MACD

The MACD is one of the most popular technical tools that you will encounter when studying trading analysis. This method is named after its creators: Gerald Appel and Stan Weinstein; it was created as a trend-following momentum indicator. The MACD indicator consists of two different types of lines: a signal line and a moving average line; these are used to calculate the difference between these two lines, based on which prices are being found.

Some investors like to use the charting method. When you do this, you will need to place a ruler on the chart to indicate time; after that, all that is left is to identify peaks and troughs based on the visible waves on the chart. You'll also be able to identify a starting point for new trends by using this technique.

Nasdaq TICK Indicator

The Nasdaq TICK indicator is one of the easiest indicators you'll encounter when dealing with trading analysis. This indicator's name comes from the ticker symbol of one of its creators: Robert D. Edwards; it is used by many traders who don't believe in using indicators at all. Because the TICK indicator was designed specifically for stocks, you will be able to identify new trends and reversals in these instruments much easier than you would with other indicators.

Relative Strength Index

The Relative Strength Index is another popular tool used by technical analysts to determine the strength of a market. Although there are several different ways of calculating this indicator, most traders will simply use the average closing price of a financial instrument over a given period along with its maximums and minimums over that period as their inputs when calculating the RSI.

Chapter 16: Trading Psychology

P sychology in Options Trading is a very important discipline to learn. I think I have some fairly unique views regarding many issues surrounding the market and trading psychology. These are my opinions and observations from over 3 years of experience in the market.

Perhaps one of the biggest mistakes' traders/investors make is they always want to buy low and sell high. They always want to be on the right side of the trade. So, if they want to make money in the market, then this is what they have to do right? This is incorrect. Many people will talk about the need to have an "aggressive" approach. There are many ways to define aggressive; however, one of the most important things that I teach my students is to trade with their discipline and trading style.

Basing your trades on emotions like fear or greed usually leads to disaster in the long run. You must have a trading plan that identifies your trading goals and objectives and have rules of entry and exit that you can stick to over time. There are several reasons why this is true. For the same reason, you may be struggling with trading:

1. Your plan is not structured enough and doesn't have enough details. It can't take into account the changes that will occur over time and attrition in the markets.

2. The plan itself has become your strategy (you are trading by the seat of your pants).

3. You continue to add to losing positions hoping to make them profitable. This is a common trait among many traders with accounts not covered by their brokerages' stop-loss provisions.

We are all human and it is very important to have a plan of action and stick to it. The reason is simple: the market does not care what you want, only what you trade. You must determine your goals and objectives when it comes to trading. These should be specific such as "I would like to make $ X over the next 1 year at least 2X a year" or "I would like to have a portfolio with at least 5% gains per month regardless of any drawdown". Then you need to structure your plan so that you will meet those goals over time. You have got to be very careful about your attitude because it will affect your performance.

This is one of the main reasons why you will often find that people who have been in a trade for a while will start to have doubts. They start to wonder if they made the right decision. Gee, if this is how I feel, then what about everyone else? Since you can't control everyone else's actions, it only makes sense that you should be very cautious with your actions. This is what we refer to as "trading psychology". Your thoughts cloud your judgment, and your actions are based on the results that you get. This creates a very powerful imbalance between your actions and reactions in terms of trade management.

Conclusion

T rading options involves a selection of considerations both before as well as after the trade has been placed. Many of the mistakes mentioned may be accounted for before the trade is opened through the use of the tools and materials. The one most significant step to trading options is developing a scheme as well as stick with it!

In this book, you find several of the equipment as well as materials that will help you build your plan. Make use of these along with other trading programs and resources Fidelity offers to allow you to stay away from these typical choices trading mistakes.

Once again, day trading is not for everybody. However, based upon hard-won, individual experience, this book provides you with the details you require to see if day trading is an excellent individual option for you on your journey to monetary liberty and security.

This manual offers you the type of standard detailed details you've been trying to find to make an educated choice about day trading. Make no error about it; this kind of speculative stock trading is not for everybody. By setting out the procedure you require to go through in a practical and useful method, you get a clear concept of precisely what you'll be entering when you begin day trading.

Far from dissuading or downhearted, it also provides a practical and well-balanced view of what it's like to prepare to trade, in addition to the truths you'll deal with when you day trade. You get vital pointers on the state of minds you require to embrace, the tools you need to get, crucial strategies effective and reliable day traders utilize, and directions on how to establish your extremely own effective individual day-trading method.

You are looking at the best manuscript if you are a total rookie to day trading and desire the within dope or straight talk about this kind of securities trading. Rather of investing an excessive quantity of time and volume area on just how much you can make from day trading, in addition to the monetary liberty you can delight in, this manuscript focuses the majority of its firepower on what you require to understand so you can be successful with day trading.

One of my favorite things about options is that you can get involved in options trading without having much money. If people were smart and disciplined about it, options trading could even provide a way out of a low-income situation. You can start trading with a hundred dollars, and if you are careful with it a year from now, there is no reason that you could not significantly grow that into a large trading account.

Just remember that options trading is a serious business, but it can be fun and exciting too. There is no reason why making money has to be tedious and difficult. You can get involved at the highest levels of our economy with the best companies by trading options. You will be able to go by on the stock market and earn some of your profits.